Why Noah Chose the Dove

Isaac Bashevis Singer

Why Noah Chose the Dove
Pictures by Eric Carle

Translated by Elizabeth Shub

SCHOLASTIC INC.
New York Toronto London Auckland Sydney
Mexico City New Delhi Hong Kong

When the people sinned and God decided to punish them by sending the flood, all the animals gathered around Noah's ark. Noah was a righteous man, and God had told him how to save himself and his family by building an ark that would float and shelter them when the waters rose.

The animals had heard a rumor that Noah was to take with him on the ark only the best of all the living creatures. So the animals came and vied with one another, each boasting about its own virtues and whenever possible belittling the merits of others.

The lion roared: "I am
the strongest of all the
beasts, and I surely must be saved."
The elephant blared:
"I am the largest. I have the
longest trunk, the biggest ears,
and the heaviest feet."

"To be big and heavy
is not so important,"
yapped the fox. "I,
the fox, am the cleverest
of all."

"What about me?"
brayed the donkey.
"I thought I was the
cleverest."

"It seems anyone can
be clever," yipped the
skunk. "I smell the best
of all the animals. My
perfume is famous."

"All of you scramble over
the earth, but I'm the only
one that can climb trees,"
shrieked the monkey.

"The only one!" growled
the bear. "What do you
think I do?"

"And how about me?"
chattered the squirrel
indignantly.

"I belong to the tiger family," purred the cat.
"I'm a cousin of the elephant," squeaked the mouse.

"I'm just as strong as
the lion," snarled the tiger.
"And I have the most
beautiful fur."

"My spots are more
admired than your stripes,"
the leopard spat back.

"I am man's closest friend," yelped the dog.

"You're no friend. You're just a fawning flatterer," bayed the wolf. "I am proud. I'm a lone wolf and flatter no one."

"Baa!" blatted the sheep. "That's why you're always hungry. Give nothing, get nothing. I give man my wool, and he takes care of me."

"You give man
wool, but I give him sweet
honey," droned the bee.
"Besides, I have venom
to protect me from my
enemies."

"What is your venom
compared with mine?"
rattled the snake. "And
I am closer to
Mother Earth than
any of you."

"Not as close as I am," protested the earthworm, sticking its head out of the ground.

"I lay eggs," clucked the hen.

"I give milk," mooed the cow.

"I help man plow the
earth," bellowed the ox.

"I carry man," neighed the horse. "And I have the largest eyes of all of you."

"You have the largest eyes, but you have only two, while I have many," the house fly buzzed right into the horse's ear.

"Compared with me, you're all midgets." The giraffe's words came from a distance as he nibbled the leaves off the top of a tree.

"I'm almost as tall as you are," chortled the camel. "And I can travel in the desert for days without food or water."

"You two are tall, but I'm fat," snorted the hippopotamus. "And I'm pretty sure that my mouth is bigger than anybody's."

"Don't be so sure," snapped the crocodile, and yawned.

"I can speak like a human," squawked the parrot.

"You don't really speak. You just imitate," the rooster crowed. "I know only one word, 'cock-a-doodle-doo,' but it is my own."

"I see with my ears;
I fly by hearing," piped the bat.
"I sing with my wing,"
chirped the cricket.

There were many more creatures who were eager to praise themselves. But Noah had noticed that the dove was perched alone on a branch and did not try to speak and compete with the other animals.

"Why are you silent?" Noah asked the dove. "Don't you have anything to boast about?"

"I don't think of myself as better or wiser or more attractive than the other animals," cooed the dove. "Each one of us has something the other doesn't have, given us by God who created us all."

"The dove is right," Noah said. "There is no need to boast and compete with one another. God has ordered me to take creatures of all kinds into the ark, cattle and beast, bird and insect."

The animals were overjoyed when they heard these words, and all their grudges were forgotten.

Before Noah opened the door of the ark, he said: "I love all of you, but because the dove remained modest and silent while the rest of you bragged and argued, I choose it to be my messenger."

Noah kept his word. When the rains stopped, he sent the dove to fly over the world and bring back news of how things were. At last she returned with an olive leaf in her beak, and Noah knew that the waters had receded. When the land finally became dry, Noah and his family and all the animals left the ark.

After the flood God promised that never again would he destroy the earth because of man's sins, and that seed time and harvest, cold and heat, summer and winter, day and night would never cease.

The truth is that there are in the world more doves than there are tigers, leopards, wolves, vultures, and other ferocious beasts. The dove lives happily without fighting. It is the bird of peace.

ISBN 0-590-99455-7

Text copyright © 1973 by Isaac Bashevis Singer. Pictures copyright © 1974 by Eric Carle. All rights reserved. Published by Scholastic Inc., 555 Broadway, New York, NY 10012, by arrangement with Farrar, Straus and Giroux . SCHOLASTIC and associated logos are trademarks and/or registered trademarks of Scholastic Inc.

12 11 10 9 8 7 6   6 7 8 9/0

Printed in the U.S.A.   08

First Scholastic printing, April 2001